Carl Eickemeyer, Lilian Westcott Eickemeyer

Among the Pueblo Indians

Carl Eickemeyer, Lilian Westcott Eickemeyer
Among the Pueblo Indians
ISBN/EAN: 9783337305086
Printed in Europe, USA, Canada, Australia, Japan
Cover: Foto ©Andreas Hilbeck / pixelio.de

More available books at **www.hansebooks.com**

Among the Pueblo Indians

BY

CARL EICKEMEYER

AND

LILIAN WESTCOTT EICKEMEYER

Illustrated with Photographs Taken by the Authors

NEW YORK
THE MERRIAM COMPANY
67 Fifth Avenue

To

THE MEMORY OF OUR FATHER

RUDOLF EICKEMEYER

THIS VOLUME

IS LOVINGLY DEDICATED

CONTENTS.

	PAGE
TO SAN ILDEFONSO,	11
FIVE DAYS IN COCHITI,	57
LIFE AT SANTO DOMINGO,	107
TAOS,	135

LIST OF ILLUSTRATIONS.

	PAGE
THE TRAVELLERS,	*Frontispiece.*
THE OUTFIT,	15
BED OF THE TESUQUE,	19
MEXICAN SETTLEMENT,	23
SAN ILDEFONSO PUEBLO,	27
MESQUITE IN BLOOM,	31
ESTUFA AT SAN ILDEFONSO,	35
PLANTING DANCE,	39
VIEW FROM THE DIVIDE,	43
NOON-DAY CAMP,	47
CAMP ON THE MESA,	51
DESCENDING FROM THE MESA,	55
MRS. JUAN DE JESUS HERRARA,	61
GALLO,	65
GALLO,	69
JUAN,	73
SCHOOL-HOUSE AT COCHITI,	77
SCHOOL-CHILDREN,	83
COCHITI INDIAN,	93

List of Illustrations.

	PAGE
PRIMITIVE PLOUGHS, .	. 99
PENA BLANCA CHURCH, .	. 103
CORRAL AT SANTO DOMINGO,	. 111
A STREET IN SANTO DOMINGO,	. 115
IN HOLIDAY ATTIRE, .	. 119
INDIAN HOME,	. 123
IN THE CAÑON, .	. 131
IN THE FIELDS, .	. 139
WEARY OF WORK,	. 143
FATHER AND SON,	. 147
TAOS BUCKS,	. 151
TAOS PUEBLO, .	. 155
ESTUFA AT TAOS, .	. 159
RUINS OF THE CHURCH,	. 163
TAOS INDIAN,	. 167
TAOS CHURCH, . .	. 171
RETURNING FROM THE FIELDS,	. 175
INDIAN PLOUGH TEAM,	. 179
ASTRAY, . .	. 183
A YOUTHFUL DANCER, .	. 187
NAVAJOES, ...	. 191

I.
TO SAN ILDEFONSO.

TO SAN ILDEFONSO.

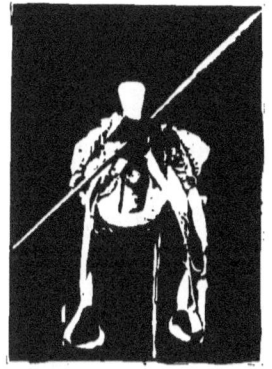
ON a spring evening, just at sunset, the little Western train landed us in quaint old Santa Fé, the city of the Holy Faith. Around the door of the station some Mexicans were loitering in their usual lazy fashion, as they watched the passengers alight and enter stages in waiting to take them to the hotels. Then, their curiosity being satisfied, they lapsed into their former state of indifference and waited for the next excitement.

We had journeyed from New York to New Mexico for the purpose of visiting the Pueblo Indians, and for a day or two after our arrival in Santa Fé were kept busy preparing for the Indian trip, which we decided to take in a prairie schooner, such as the early Western settlers used in travelling from place to place. This wagon was obtained from an old Jew, from whom we also hired two horses, whose appearance at the start indicated they would be unable to finish the trip. We were assured, however, that they would carry us through, in spite of their protruding teeth, prominent ribs, and swollen knee-joints, which seemed to point to the contrary. Our wagon was loaded with a little camp stove and cooking utensils, two cameras, a bag filled with provisions, and a bag containing blankets. These necessary articles, together with a collection of firearms, completed our outfit and gave us an air of comfort as well as safety.

Thus equipped, the journey began about five o'clock on a beautiful morning, leaving the old town, with its sleeping inhabitants, in the distance, as we travelled on toward the north, hoping to reach San Ildefonso, a pueblo about twenty-seven miles from Santa Fe, ere nightfall.

The road over which we passed during the day had on either side deep arroyos formed by heavy rainfalls which come suddenly in cloud-bursts, washing out in

THE OUTFIT.

To San Ildefonso.

the soil deep gullies with perpendicular sides twenty feet or more in depth. Along the roadside and back through the country grew the scrub cedar with its tiny berries and rich green coloring. Sage bushes of a lighter green, and little clumps of buffalo grass, sprang up here and there, giving a grayish cast to the whole country.

We jogged slowly along toward the divide which forms the watershed between the Pecos and the upper portion of the Rio Grande, and when that point was reached such a picture was presented to our enraptured gaze as is seldom seen, and when once seen is never forgotten. Looking northward, lofty hills stood out in bold relief, the brighter coloring of those in the foreground gradually fading into the delicate opalescent tints of those near the horizon, where they seemed to pale and fade away in the cloudless blue of the summer sky. To the eastward the Santa Fé Mountains, with their gorgeous coloring and snow-tipped peaks extending far into the blue ether, formed a breastwork over which the morning sun gradually rose, shedding a golden glory over the country as far as the eye could scan. To the west, and rivalling in

Among the Pueblo Indians.

beauty those at our right hand, extended in unbroken line the Jamez Mountains, with purple bases, and delicate blue tips reaching far into the unfathomable sky.

Following the Tesuque, a small stream running by the roadside, we neared the pueblo of that name; but as the population is small and the place not of special interest, our stay there was a short one, our destination being San Ildefonso, some distance further north. Beyond Tesuque were several small Mexican settlements, their one-story adobe houses so near the color of the soil as to be almost imperceptible until one is close upon them. Surrounding some of these houses were prosperous fruit ranches, obtaining moisture from esaques, or irrigating ditches, which carry the water of the neighboring mountain streams and rivers into the ranches, and take the place of rain, which is seldom seen in this part of the country. Along the roadside, here and there, were small wooden crosses upheld by stones piled one upon the other. These crosses, we afterward learned, marked the places where coffins had been rested while being carried from the houses to their final resting-places.

We neared San Ildefonso a little after noon, and on

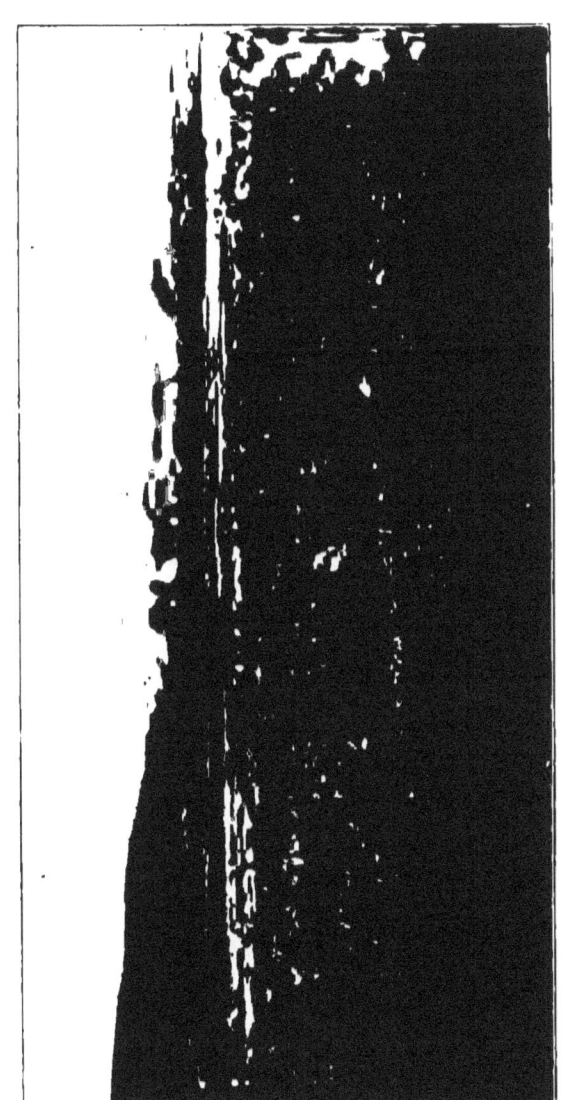

BED OF THE TESUQUE.

To San Ildefonso.

the outskirts of the pueblo saw many Indians in bright-colored garments, ploughing in the fields. They presented a most picturesque appearance, moving in and out among the young corn, driving yokes of oxen drawing primitive Indian ploughs. Others were at work on the esaques that supply the fields with water. The construction of these irrigating ditches takes considerable time, skill, and much labor, as they sometimes carry water from mountain streams many miles away to the section under cultivation. They are, therefore, made quite deep and very narrow, to allow as little loss of water by evaporation as possible. The fields are flooded once a week, and seemed to be in a most flourishing condition.

Proceeding a little farther, we entered the sunny, dusty plaza, lined on all sides by the typical Indian home, a two-story adobe house, the second story setting a little back and having the roof of the first as a sort of front yard. Most of these houses are entered by small doors leading from the plaza into a large front room, though some Indians retain the old custom which existed when the pueblos were attacked by wandering tribes of Apaches and Navajoes that

Among the Pueblo Indians.

roamed through the country, giving the peaceful village Indians much anxiety and fear for their safety. They consequently have no doors to their houses, but enter the lower rooms through a hatchway in the roof. In front of all the houses are rudely constructed ladders, by means of which access is gained to the upper rooms, and up these rickety ladders children of all ages and sizes ascend, those of a larger growth carrying on their backs little ones whose mothers feel not the slightest anxiety as they view from a distance the perilous ascent.

We drove to the home of a thrifty Indian who speaks fairly well the English language, and were most cordially greeted by his wife, who, on seeing our approach, hastened down the ladder to welcome us. On entering the abode the first objects noticed were the pictures that hung on the white walls of the rooms. They were of a purely religious nature, representing Christ, the Virgin Mary, and the Saints. They were painted on wood and were brought from Mexico many years ago. So old are they that they have become dimmed and faded by the ravages of time, but are none the less sacred in the eyes of the

MEXICAN SETTLEMENT.

To San Ildefonso.

owner on that account. In a back room, which is the living room of the family, were two fire-places. One of these was assigned to us, while in the other our hostess prepared her noonday meal of tortillas, dried beef, and coffee. It was a most interesting sight to see her seated before the little corner fire-place making tortillas, a concoction of flour and water mixed together and kneaded as our bread is. When it was considered the right consistence, it was rolled out in flat round discs like pancakes and cooked on a piece of stone upheld by an iron tripod over a blazing wood fire. They required several turnings, and when finished we were presented with a sample of the morning's baking, but the toughened mass was not very palatable. We in turn gave them some of our provisions, which they ate with a keen relish as they sat on the hard cemented floor in a semicircle.

After enjoying our meal, we decided to go the rounds of the pueblo and see the various places of interest to be found there. Our host conducted us first to the estufa, or council house, situated just outside the main plaza. It is here that all important questions are decided and where the Indians practise for

Among the Pueblo Indians.

their dances. The estufa, like the other houses in the pueblo, is made of adobe, but unlike them, being circular in form, it is a conspicuous figure in the village. The building is lighted only by means of an opening in the roof. This opening also serves as entrance to the place. Having climbed the steps that lead to the roof, we entered through the hatchway and descended by a ladder, the poles of which protruded high above the building. All that could be seen in the dimly-lighted room was the fire-place, in the centre directly under the ladder, and an adobe settee projecting from the wall of the building. Finding very little of interest in the bare, dark room, we wended our way in the direction of the home of the governor to pay our respects to that celebrity.

He was seated in the front room of his little house, busily engaged making moccasins. We watched him for some time at this humble occupation, greatly interested in his work. He pierced small holes in the soles, and corresponding ones in the uppers, through which he ran pieces of sinew. The bead work for which the Indian is famous is done in a similar way.

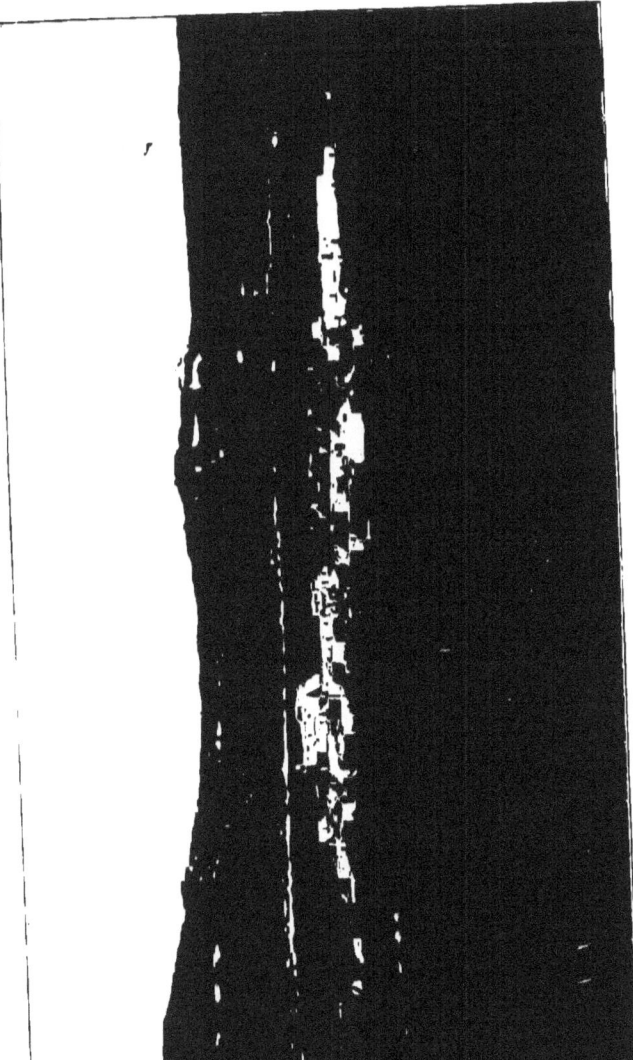

SAN ILDEFONSO PUEBLO.

To San Ildefonso.

When we had become well versed in the art of shoe-making, the governor left his work and took us into an inner room, where his wife was grinding wheat. She was kneeling before a slanting stone slab, and with a small oblong-shaped stone in her hand she rubbed the wheat between the two in a way similar to rubbing clothes on a washboard. This work is always done by the women.

By the aid of our interpreter quite a lengthy conversation was carried on with the governor, in which the affairs of the pueblo were discussed. The government was one of the first subjects inquired into, and we were greatly surprised to find such a complex form existing. It is twofold in character, resembling both the monarchial and republican. The former is exemplified in the office of cacique, or chief, who was originally appointed for life by the governor of New Mexico, to be succeeded by his eldest son. The latter, or republican form, is shown by the annual election of a governor and twelve councilmen, whose business it is to direct the affairs of the pueblo and to decide all important questions that may arise. They are second in authority only to the cacique, who has

Among the Pueblo Indians.

power to veto any decision not to his liking. The officer next in power is the fiscal, who looks after the religious affairs of the pueblo, and instructs the boys and girls in the tenets of Catholicism. He is appointed by the cacique, whose duty it also is to nominate three candidates for the office of governor and three for that of war chief, one of whom, in each case, is elected by the people to fill the office. The duty of the war chief is similar to that of our police justice. He has power to decide all questions of right and wrong that may arise, and to impose a fine of grain or money upon the offender, according to the magnitude of the offence. The election of governor, councilmen and war chief takes place each year at harvest time in the estufa, where the men and all boys capable of working in the fields congregate to vote orally for their favorite candidates.

We were, of course, anxious to attend a business meeting and see the Indian conduct it, but they are very reticent concerning their council meetings, never allowing outsiders to be present. Seeing our disappointment, the governor sought to conciliate us by inviting us to be present that evening to witness the

MESQUITE IN BLOOM.

To San Ildefonso.

practice for a dance which was to take place the following morning in the plaza.

Dancing is one of the principal pastimes of the Indian and one very often indulged in, so that any one, making even a limited stay at a pueblo, is likely to witness this most interesting sight before his departure.

When the time arrived to join the dancers, we walked toward the estufa, where the smoke and light from the camp-fire below could be seen coming out of the roof through the hatchway. The bucks were chanting, and the beating of the drum to give the dancers time reached us with muffled sound. Following our guide up the steps, we descended the ladder through clouds of smoke and found ourselves in the midst of the august assemblage. It was hard to imagine that the room, with the dim light from the camp-fire shining on the grotesque forms of the dancers, was the same we had visited during the afternoon, so great was the difference in its appearance. On the adobe settee sat the squaws, their papooses either in their arms or wrapped in blankets lying on the floor at their feet. The old bucks were

Among the Pueblo Indians.

seated on the floor in two lines opposite each other, with the drummer at their head facing the fire. The younger bucks or warriors, and the squaws, formed in line two abreast: first two bucks, then two squaws, and so on, dancing to the time given by the drummer and the chanters. The scene presented was ghostly, the dimly-lighted, smoky atmosphere giving a certain weirdness to the shadowy moving forms.

As the dance progressed some of the children, who dance quite as earnestly as their parents, joined in, and young and old went through the movements with great activity. The time of the dancing is regular for intervals, then there will be one or two beats left out, the dancers all the while keeping time perfectly with their feet. When the line, headed by two of the most athletic bucks, had encircled the hall, the two lines faced each other, spread out, crossed over, then swung around and returned to their original positions. There is quite a perceptible difference in the dancing of the buck and squaw: the former lifts his feet high from the ground as he goes through the tiresome motions that constitute his part of the programme, while the squaw simply shuffles her feet along, sway-

ESTUFA AT SAN ILDEFONSO.

ing her body from side to side, and holding out her hands as if offering something in prayer.

The dance practice was over at midnight, when, well pleased with the novel entertainment, we returned to the prairie schooner which had been drawn up in front of the house in which our dinner had been cooked at the little corner fire-place.

Soon all was still, and sleep reigned throughout the pueblo. On returning from the estufa the dancers had wearily thrown themselves down on pallets that lay on the ground in front of the houses where the other members of their families were already resting, with the deep blue star-lit sky overhead for a canopy. Slowly the waning moon rose in all the majesty of her silvery beauty, and as the mellow rays of light touched the prostrate forms of the sleepers, they seemed to work a perfect transformation, softening the hard lines on many faces.

We were awakened next morning at sunrise by the governor as he stood in the centre of the plaza calling to the people to prepare for the dance to take place directly after breakfast. Immediately all was astir, as those who were to take part in the festivity hastened to attire themselves in suitable costume. In a short time gaudily-arrayed figures appeared on the scene, coming first from one house, then from another, and wended their way in the direction of the estufa, where the participants congregated previous to their appearance in the plaza.

When the dancers had collected and the word was given to start, the first set, about thirty in number, filed from the estufa into the plaza, marching in lines two abreast. They were followed by a band of chanters, consisting of the bucks who were too old to dance. The dancers were beautifully decorated. The bucks were stripped to the waist, their hands and part of the forearms painted white, from which ran a line of white spots to the shoulder, and then down to the small of the back, resembling the fallow deer. On the upper part of the arms were armlets of rawhide, also painted white, through which were stuck green sprigs of the cottonwood tree. Around the waist was a white belt or sash of wool, having large tassels on the ends, and holding in place an embroidered skirt reaching nearly to the knee. White knee breeches were worn under the skirt. Around the left leg was

PLANTING DANCE

To San Ildefonso.

a band of worsted tied in a bow, and around the right a string of bells. From the back of the belt hung the skin of the red fox. White moccasins, with a decoration of skunk skin at the heel, completed the costume. Each carried in his right hand rattles made from gourds which grow wild in large quantities near the Indian villages; and in the left, branches of the cottonwood tree.

The squaw wore a head decoration of peculiar design, made of a thin flat board, in shape similar to the façade of the Indian church. It had three serrated vertical projections, with an open space in the centre as if for a bell. It was painted white, with borders of green and yellow, and from the peaks floated the feathers of the wild turkey. The dress was of black woollen material, and hung a little below the knee. It was gathered over the right shoulder and again under the left arm, leaving the arms and one shoulder bare. A woollen belt of unique design and bright coloring offset the costume and relieved the blackness of the dress.

On the arrival of the dancers in the plaza, the drummer took position beside them, and at his rear

Among the Pueblo Indians.

stood the group of chanters facing one another. The dance, which was much the same as that of the night before, had not progressed far when another set of about the same number filed into the plaza from the other end of the pueblo and went through the same performance.

We spent the remainder of the day taking photographs of the place and of some of the people, and in walking to an old butte, where, it is claimed, the pueblo was originally situated; but like the old cliff dwellings, the former homes of the Pueblo Indians, the place was deserted. It could be seen, however, from arrowheads and old pieces of pottery found there, that at some remote period, during the prehistoric ages, the place must have been inhabited.

During the evening we had several callers, among whom was a young Indian of good type, who could speak English as well as Spanish and his native Indian language. It is a curious fact that the language spoken in pueblos situated within a short distance of each other differs, while sometimes in two, many miles apart, the same is spoken. Fortunately all the Pueblo Indians speak Spanish, so that they

VIEW FROM THE DIVIDE.

To San Ildefonso.

may converse one with the other, even though their native languages be different. Being in doubt as to whether the pueblos we intended visiting had English-speaking Indians, we decided to take, as interpreter, Juan, the young Indian, who seemed delighted with the idea of making a third to our party. He told us he had made several trips to the different pueblos and had at one time spent a year among the Utes, whose customs he still followed. His long black hair was parted in Ute style, and on special occasions he used quite a quantity of war paint. He was unmarried, but told us he expected to take the all-important step at harvest time, when he would have saved five dollars, the amount necessary to pay the Mexican priest to perform the ceremony. The prospect of earning the five dollars and winning the maid before harvest time probably made the parting with her less hard. Whether that were the case or not, there were no tears or sad looks either from Juan or his lady love when we left San Ildefonso the following day, just as the sun rose over the little village.

The morning was beautiful. At our right, and run-

Among the Pueblo Indians.

ning by the pueblo, the Rio Grande flowed, the clear sparkling water dancing in the sunlight as it hurried on in its course through the cañon to the gulf. A soft mist seemed to overhang the neighboring hills like a mantle of gauze, through which the varied tints shone in subdued coloring and ethereal beauty.

We started through Alamo cañon, which runs parallel with White Rock cañon, containing the bed of the Rio Grande. The two are divided in places by high ledges of rock, the top of which, for about a thickness of one hundred feet, is of volcanic origin; and below it are strata of different kinds of rock, sand, and clay, varying from white to light red and blue, with all the intervening shades so perfectly blended as to make it impossible to detect the joining of one color with another. The rocks average in height about three hundred feet, and above them, on the west, tower the San Ildefonso range, where the Indian boys from the pueblo hunt deer and antelope.

The trip up the cañon was like driving through a park; the cactus in bloom with its yellow, white and red flowers, and the valley covered with fragrant balsam, sage bushes, and clumps of buffalo grass. There

NOON-DAY CAMP.

To San Ildefonso.

was good shooting all the way, the cotton-tails and wild doves being plentiful, while an occasional jack rabbit ran in and out among the sage bushes, giving us a lively chase for him.

About noon we struck camp just off the road. After unloading the wagon and setting up the little stove, Juan started up the cañon toward the Rio Grande for water. He had been gone but a short time when a strange noise was heard. Gradually the sound came nearer, and coming toward us, down the cañon, was a flock of goats, sheep and lambs, driven by a Mexican. The driver could not speak our language nor we his, but by signs he was made to understand that we wanted to purchase a lamb, and he seemed very willing to let us have one. When Juan returned with the water he played the part of butcher, killing and dressing the lamb and preparing it to be cooked. Soon dinner was on the fire, and in about twenty minutes from the time the lamb was running around we were eating him.

Our camp for the night was behind a clump of trees, near the narrow-gauge railroad which runs through this part of the country; and after supper

Among the Pueblo Indians.

our bed in the wagon was prepared by spreading a pair of blankets on the floor for a mattress, and using a pair for covering—then, putting the canvas wagon cover over the hoops, the bed was ready for us. We tied the horses to a tree near by, and entered our sleeping apartment, while Juan, wrapping his blanket around him, lay on the ground by the side of the wagon.

We arose at sunrise next morning, and, after enjoying our breakfast of lamb, potatoes and coffee, journeyed upward through a very rough and mountainous country, broken up by high hills and deep arroyos. About noon we struck camp on the dusty road beside a little Mexican settlement. An old Mexican, who brought us some water, sat beside the fence watching us prepare dinner, which we ate sitting under the wagon, to protect us from the heat of the sun.

Beyond this settlement a steep hill led to the bare and barren mesa, where there was not even a sage bush in sight. Prairie on all sides of us, and we, like tiny specks upon a great ocean, sailed on and on with nothing visible but prairie and sky. Slowly the sun

CAMP ON THE MESA.

To San Ildefonso.

rode on in glory toward the west, and, as it sank to rest below the horizon, twinkling stars came out one by one, until the sky, that a short time before was all aglow with the sun's roseate rays, was illumined by the lesser light of the stars, which looked protectingly down on us as we slept. During the night the wind came up and blew across the prairie with terrific force, almost taking the wagon cover with it in its mad sweep over the mesa, and it was not until the cover had been tied down with a strong rope that we felt at all secure. Then, pinning a mackintosh over the opening at the foot to keep the wind out, we tried to settle ourselves, but it was not possible to sleep long. As there were no trees around, the horses had to be tied to the back of the wagon, and first one, then the other, would jar it, while occasionally a horse's head was thrust under the cover as he tried to get at our feet. Next morning the mackintosh that had been used as a curtain was found chewed into ribbons, and the horse had quieted down.

Our supply of water was so low that there was very little coffee for breakfast, and we dispensed altogether with our usual morning's ablution, a ceremony we were often obliged to omit during the trip. However, Juan assured us he could get water a little way down the road, but, after driving on hour after hour and still no water, we began to doubt his knowledge of the country. Still he persisted, "It is right down there."

The Indian has no idea of distance. One time, when asked how far a certain place was, Juan replied, "Three days with burros and one day with a horse." Our hope now was that our distance from water would not be reckoned with burros, for as the sun shone more brightly our thirst became almost unbearable. Still we drove on, and no water.

Our descent from the mesa to the plain below was over a steep, narrow and rough road winding around the edge of a cliff about nine hundred feet in height. Applying the brakes, we reached the foot in safety, and to our great joy and relief a tiny stream was running along by the roadside. We arrived here just in time, for the little stream gradually grew less and less, and then vanished altogether. Juan told us it would appear again next morning, and that this was quite a common occurrence.

DESCENDING FROM THE MESA.

II.

FIVE DAYS IN COCHITI.

SAN JUAN'S DAY.

OUR arrival at Cochiti, late in the afternoon, was witnessed by several squaws of the village, who were filling water jars down at the rio. They paused in their work as we drew near and forded the river, greeting us in the usual friendly manner; then, with their burdens skilfully balanced on their heads, they passed on up the sandy hill that forms the approach to the little settlement.

Half-way up the hill were fruit orchards, in the corners of which were cribs built on the ends of long poles. They looked like small rustic summer houses; but instead of being used for pleasure, they were guard-houses, where some of the men keep watch at night over the fruit near by.

Among the Pueblo Indians.

Cochiti has a population of nearly four hundred Indians and about half as many Mexicans. It is the only pueblo we visited having a Mexican settlement, it being contrary to the wishes of the Government to have the two races quartered together. But somehow or other the Mexican element has worked its way into Cochiti, and in several instances the Indian and Mexican have intermarried, making the separation of the races impossible.

Juan conducted us to the home of a friend—Juan de Jesus Herrara—who with his family, consisting of an aged father and mother, a wife and three children, lived in the little adobe house that for the following few days was our home. One of the two rooms on the ground floor was assigned to us for use as a bedroom, kitchen and reception-room during our stay. We spread the blankets on the floor in one corner, and our bedroom was ready for use; lighting a fire on the hearth and preparing our evening meal made the kitchen a reality, while entertaining half a dozen old bucks and squaws who had been drawn to the spot out of curiosity gave the place quite the air of a reception-room.

MRS. JUAN DE JESUS HERRARA.

San Juan's Day.

Our visitors seated themselves on the floor, watching us prepare supper. Unfortunately we could not converse with them, as they could not speak English, and Juan, our interpreter, had gone out to see the place and to make friends among the Indians. It was a strange sight. The little cellar-like room had only the light of a single candle shining dimly through it, and the smoke from cigarettes the bucks were enjoying made the forms appear almost ghostly in their indistinctness. When our visitors had partaken of crackers and coffee, their curiosity being fully, and their appetites partially, satisfied, they left.

We retired early, but the place was so noisy that it was impossible to sleep. At sundown the church bell had rung for about an hour, after which a shotgun was fired in the plaza. More bell-ringing followed, and the gun was fired twice; still more bell-ringing, and the gun was fired a third time. This alternate ringing and firing, together with violin-playing by some Mexicans who wandered through the plaza, making noisy demonstrations all the while, ushered in San Juan's Day; and at daybreak the following morning (Sunday) the whole community were ready to participate in the celebration.

The little adobe church with its wooden cross was the scene of the earliest activity, as old and young, Indian and Mexican, wended their way in the direction of the sanctuary to be present at mass, conducted by a Mexican priest from a neighboring town.

We entered with the rest, and found ourselves in a large, bare room with cemented floor, on which there were no seats. The side walls of the church were adorned from door to altar with small crosses, between which had been placed alternately candlesticks and pictures of the saints. On either side of the altar were paintings of Christ, considered of great value, and claimed to have been brought from Mexico hundreds of years ago. On the altar, which is surrounded by a wooden railing of rude workmanship, were candles and images of the saints.

We were greatly interested to see what the ingenuity of the Indian had accomplished in the art of interior church decoration. On the rafters were placed good-sized logs, faced off, the flat side being turned

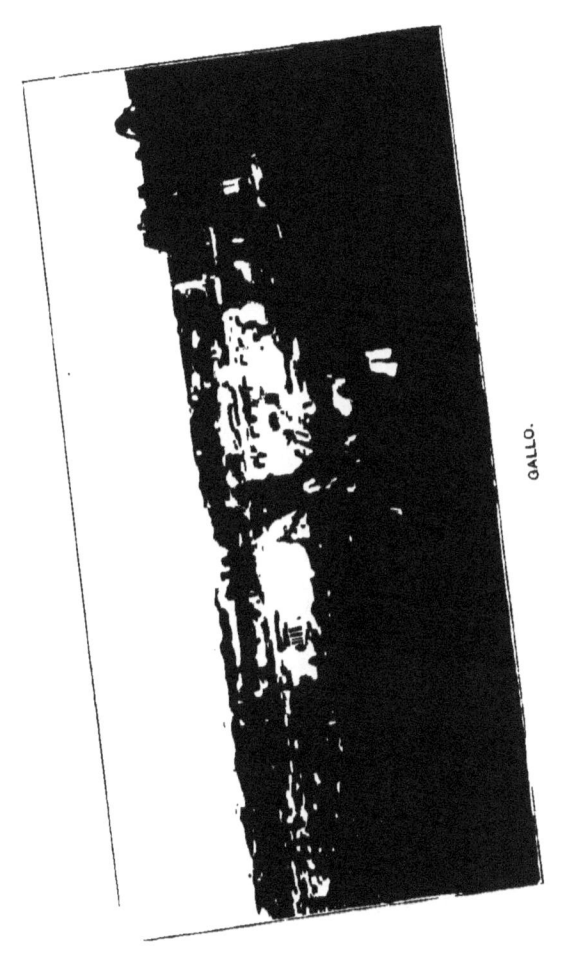

GALLO.

San Juan's Day.

down, and on this flattened surface were original characteristic paintings and drawings of bear and buffalo hunted by Indians. The dimly-lighted church with its close atmosphere had a sepulchral appearance, and we were glad to get once more in the open air and leave the Indian to hear mass.

Later during the morning, going into the governor's house, we came suddenly upon a most interesting sight. In the centre of the room, which had been cleared of everything but an olla of water, sat seventeen bucks, forming a circle. They were singing in a sort of nasal twang, and at our entrance kept on with the inharmonious strains, not so much as looking at us. One of the bucks had a drum resembling a good-sized cask. These drums are made from solid pieces of wood, which the Indians hollow out and tightly draw drumheads of sheepskin over the ends. Opposite the drummer sat the war chief, a vicious-looking fellow, wearing a belt of Winchester cartridges. He sat there erectly, not a muscle in his body moving except those he necessarily used in producing the nasal twang that constituted the song. All the while they smoked cigarettes rolled in corn husks, the smoking not interfering in the least with the singing.

They sang thus until noon, when it was time to prepare for the games which were to take place in the plaza after dinner. The festivities began with the celebrated game of gallo, which was most thoroughly enjoyed by all but the poor rooster, whose unearthly cries elicited not the slightest feeling of sympathy among the many spectators assembled on the housetops near by, keenly enjoying the cruel sport and eagerly applauding when a good point was made by the contestants. Every young Indian and Mexican who could procure a horse of any kind joined in the game. It was played by two at a time, an Indian and a Mexican evenly matched. The two came together in the centre of the plaza, where a live rooster was brought, his feet tied together with rawhide. Each took hold of one of the legs, and, at the word given by the governor of the pueblo, pulled, trying to get possession of the bird, which all the while was screeching as if in terrible agony. The contestants violently swayed from side to side, pulling with all their strength. Finally, the Indian gained an advantage,

San Juan's Day.

and, spurring his pony, ran off with the rooster, nearly dragging his opponent from his horse, amid wild shouts from the excited spectators on the roofs. It seemed as if the bird must be torn apart, but, besides losing its breath and a few feathers, it stood the ordeal very well.

The Mexican then rode to the centre of the plaza and faced the audience, while the Indian started at one end with the rooster in his right hand. He rode by the Mexican at full speed, and in passing struck him over the head with it. The Mexican tried to catch the bird, but failed. They fought in this way for some time, until both were covered with feathers and blood from the now lifeless rooster, but neither seemed to gain much advantage both being exhausted. The rest of the horsemen standing near, wishing for a chance, rode up and separated them. In the break which followed, the one with the rooster started off at full speed for his home, closely followed by the rest of the horsemen, who tried to get possession of it, but he succeeded in reaching home without parting company with the poor lifeless thing, thus becoming

Among the Pueblo Indians.

the happy possessor of the bird and the victor of the game.

Another game was started by two others, and so on until each had a chance to wrestle for a rooster, which in some cases passed through many hands before it was finally won. The programme was carried out systematically, as if it had been carefully prepared.

After finishing the game of gallo the horsemen lined up one by one and rode by another live rooster that had been placed in sand with only his head in sight. The idea was to pick him up while riding by. Each rider eagerly watched the others as they reached from the saddle and tried to catch the bird. Finally one succeeded, and, grasping the head, ran off with the rooster, followed by all the horsemen. He rode out of the plaza and over the prairie, up deep arroyos, and back through the several streets of the pueblo, in his efforts to elude his followers, and, reaching home with it, the bird was his.

Next in order came foot races by some of the young bucks, after which some girls tried their skill at running.

It being San Juan's Day, every one by the name of

JUAN.

San Juan's Day.

Juan was obliged to contribute something to be given to the people. Accordingly all articles were carried to the roof of one of the houses near by, and thrown down, one by one, into the crowd assembled below. Juan, possessing the name of the day, was told he must make a contribution as the others of that name did. Accordingly he took some birds he had previously shot for our supper, and carried them to the house-top. All stood with upturned faces and outstretched hands as one article after another fell into some grasping palm. The collection consisted of pieces of leather, bright bits of calico, birds, and tortillas. No one became the actual owner of anything until he reached home with it, and any one who could get an article away from another before he arrived at that place of safety was privileged to do so. This ended the celebration, and at sundown San Juan's Day was over.

A VISIT TO THE SCHOOL-HOUSE.

At sunrise the following morning the governor called loudly from his position in the centre of the pueblo, assigning to the men assembled in the doorways the work they were to perform that day. As the different names were called the owners disappeared within the houses to prepare for the work allotted to them, and hurried to the scene of action to do their share of the labor.

After breakfast we decided to visit the school-house near by and see the little Indian children assembled there. Arriving early, we were most cordially welcomed by the teacher, Mrs. Grozier, of Boston, the only white woman in Cochiti.

It would be hard to find a more interesting place in the pueblo than the school-house, a one-story adobe building fitted up by the Government, under whose control the school is carried on.

Of the thirty-two pupils enrolled upon the school

SCHOOL-HOUSE AT COCHITI.

A Visit to the School-house.

register the average daily attendance is about one-half the full number. The parents of the children, not realizing the benefits to be derived from a regular attendance, keep them at home on the slightest provocation, to do any and all kinds of work. But, in spite of this drawback, the school seemed in a flourishing condition, and about nine o'clock the little barefooted, scantily-clad children were seated at desks similar to those used in any well-regulated schoolroom, ready to begin the work of the day.

While waiting for the little ones to become quiet we glanced around the room. In front, with the white wall for a background, hung the grand old Stars and Stripes, which, in spite of the dusky faces of the little ones and their unintelligible language when conversing with one another, gave us a pleasurable homelike feeling. On either side of the national emblem, and on the walls of the room, hung illustrated charts of various descriptions, to enable the little ones more readily to grasp the subjects intended for their study. On a blackboard at the left of the room was a drawing of a train of cars done by a little boy whose talent was clearly shown by this well-executed work.

Among the Pueblo Indians.

In addition to the regular attendants of the school were several squaws who dropped in from time to time during the session, probably finding the school-room, with its evenly-boarded floor and large open windows, a pleasant change from their own houses.

When the children became sufficiently subdued to give attention to the work of the day, the opening exercises began. First the Lord's prayer was repeated in English, led by the teacher, whom the children followed closely in broken accent, and with reverently bowed heads. "Come to Jesus" was sung by the school, and some little voices were very effective as they joined in the sweet strains of the old hymn with the greatest of zeal and animation. By the time the last verse was reached the room fairly rang with the enthusiastic efforts of the youthful songsters. The singing of two other pieces completed the exercises, and the children were ready to begin their lessons.

A bright little boy was called upon to read, and from his second reader selected a piece called "The Boy and the Bubbles," his Spanish accent of the English words making his rendering of the piece very interesting. Next a letter from the same book was

A Visit to the School=house.

read. It was dated "New York, December 10th, 1884," and headed "Dear Santa Claus." This being printed in script made the reading of it more difficult for the little fellow, but he got through the task very well, being helped over the harder words by his teacher.

By this time all the children were anxious to show us their accomplishments, and there were half a dozen applicants to speak a piece. A little girl of seven was chosen as elocutionist, and she recited "Little bird, little bird up in a tree," etc. When she had finished another wanted to show us how well she could speak the same piece, which it seemed they all knew. And so we again heard about "Little bird," and were as much entertained as we had been the first time.

Meanwhile many of the children had drawn pictures to which they had signed their names, and they proudly exhibited them to us, being greatly elated over any sign of approval we chanced to bestow upon them.

Just at this point in the most interesting programme the teacher was called from the room to answer some call from a needy neighbor. Instantly their studious

Among the Pueblo Indians.

manner changed for one of play, and they were once more "little Indians," laughing and talking in their wonderful threefold language, a mixture of Indian, Spanish and English, sometimes in one sentence using words from all three languages.

At one side of the room some little girls were gathered, all talking at the same time; but as they were conversing in a language unknown to us, we turned our attention to a group of four boys seated near by. They had evidently had some dispute, and seemed far from reaching an amicable settlement of the case. "I'll bet you twenty-five dollars," said our little friend, who a few minutes before had read to us. "And I've got lots of money," he continued, in earnest tones. "Then let's go and buy candy with it," said one of his more practical companions, evidently not caring to carry on the argument with such a prospect in view. Whether they bought the candy or not, we do not know, for, her mission being for the time fulfilled, the teacher returned, and order was restored out of the chaos that so recently reigned.

After this little impromptu recess the children returned to their lessons with renewed vigor, and per-

SCHOOL-CHILDREN.

A Visit to the School-house.

formed the mathematical part of the programme. Several examples were worked by all the class in addition, subtraction, and multiplication, and in most cases they were correctly done. The multiplication tables were then given by two or three of the more advanced pupils; the monotonous recital of "twice one are two," "twice two are four," etc., being given in the same monotone that children always use when wrestling with these fundamental principles of arithmetic.

At this stage of proceedings some of the babies, whom the little girls in many cases are obliged to take to school with them, began to get uneasy and long for a freedom not to be found within the walls of a school-room, and so, to pacify these little victims of early education, the teacher brought from her seemingly inexhaustible supply, some much-sought-after candy, or "coack" as it is fondly called, and quieted the little martyrs as their older and more enlightened sisters proceeded with the well-known truths, "twice three are six, twice four are eight."

The daily lessons over, school was dismissed. The children reluctantly left, those having little charges marching off with them on their backs, while those fortunate enough not to be so burdened ran off with the unrestricted freedom and joyousness of childhood.

Accepting a most cordial invitation to have lunch in the school-house, we seated ourselves at desks recently vacated by the children, and heartily enjoyed the meal cooked at the schoolroom fireplace.

Soon we heard sounds of muffled laughter, and saw popping out from under the desks the dishevelled locks of the little hero of the twenty-five dollar bet and his philosophical companion. They knew if seen at the time of dimissal they would be sent home with the rest, and so by strategy they sought to remain in school, where it seems they would rather be than anywhere else. So anxious are they to get to school that sometimes they arrive at five o'clock in the morning, much to the discomfiture of the teacher, who tells them to go home and come later; whereupon they point to the sun, thus trying to convince her that it is time to begin operations.

Our little friends, having obtained permission to remain if quiet, seated themselves on the floor in front of the room and amused themselves for some time trying to earn, by their good behavior, the right

A Visit to the School-house.

to remain within the hallowed walls. But soon their love for fun predominated, and sounds of muffled laughter proceeded from the spot the boys occupied, as a pair of mischievous black eyes looked in our direction to see if their recent outburst of hilarity was to be the cause of banishment. Instead of banishment, however, their number was reinforced. As soon as they had finished their frugal repasts, the other children wandered back in the direction of the school-house, and stood in the doorway with such longing expressions that they were allowed to enter, babies and all, and the room had much the same appearance it had had twenty minutes before. But this time they came for fun, and they had it.

During the course of the afternoon the teacher, who is obliged to minister to their bodily as well as their mental needs, had occasion to bring out her medicine case, containing many phials of sugar pills. Immediately several little hands were entreatingly outstretched, as their possessors exclaimed, in a serio-comic manner, "Mungi milo" (very sick). But judging from their healthful appearance a few moments previous to the beseeching demands, it was impossi-

Among the Pueblo Indians.

ble to convince the dispenser of the pills that an epidemic had suddenly appeared in their midst, and so, laughingly putting up her case, she gave to each little impostor some coack, and they were no more "mungi milo."

Until nearly sundown the little company remained in possession of the field, enjoying themselves as only children can; then, bidding us good-by, they disbanded, going to their several homes. And it is to be hoped, for the sake of their indulgent friend and teacher, that they did not consider the sun in the right position for them to return until long after five o'clock.

Returning to our domicile, we found Juan seated before the little window, making an elaborate toilet. A second glance revealed the fact that he was using our brush and comb to work some gun grease into his shining black locks. He was putting on the finishing touches, and seemed greatly pleased with his image reflected in a piece of broken looking-glass he carried with him. He had daubed his face with red war-paint, and the parting of his hair formed a straight line of red, from which the greasy black hair

A Visit to the School=house.

receded in a solid mass. Not in the least abashed by our presence, he took one more glance at himself in the tiny mirror, and, being satisfied with the reflection, he put the articles back in place and waited for orders.

Being too fascinated by the audacity of his act to give him the warranted reprimand, we sent Juan to shoot some birds for supper, and, between laughing and scolding, gave the articles in question a good share of soap, water and hard rubbing.

SIGHT-SEEING.

NEXT morning we went to the school-house again, to take pictures of the teacher and scholars. The children, with whom we had become great friends, were full of fun and quite willing to be photographed, probably not sharing with the older ones the superstitious idea that it would bring them harm. They lined up against the wall of the school-house, and seemed to think posing great sport. When the pictures had been taken, the little ones went back to their lessons, while we started on a purchasing expedition.

There was an old Mexican woman in the pueblo who possessed many paintings of saints, madonnas, etc., such as were in the little house at San Ildefonso. Wishing to add one or two of these to our collection of curios, we called at the house where the woman lived with her two daughters, one of whom spoke English quite well, having attend school in the pueblo.

Sight=seeing.

They brought down picture after picture, some so faded that it was almost impossible to trace even the outlines of a form. Selecting some of the better-preserved ones, we offered a fair price for them, but the old woman protested, saying she could not possibly part with them—they were sacred. A larger amount being offered she seemed more inclined to part with the sacred relics, and, when the price was raised for the last time, she gladly seized the opportunity of turning saints into gold, and sold four of them, "Dolores," "San Francisco," "San Juan," and "San Bicente."

Being highly pleased with the bargains they had made, they brought out several other articles for which they wanted exorbitant prices, but, finding we did not want them at all, they lowered their figures until it seemed as if they would give them away, so anxious were they to have us take them.

This Mexican room was very different from those in the Indian houses, resembling one that might be seen in the poorer quarters of any town. There was a rag carpet on the floor (the rooms in the Indian houses are not even boarded), and, besides several

Among the Pueblo Indians.

chairs and a table, there was a bedstead with a gaudy blanket of Mexican manufacture for a covering. The walls were covered with a cheap paper, and what struck us as being very peculiar were two frames, the faces of which were turned toward the wall. They were looking-glasses, which in the case of a death in a family are always turned toward the wall for one year.

A daughter of the old Mexican woman had died a few months previous to our arrival in the pueblo, where her funeral had been celebrated with great pomp, and it was for this girl the family were mourning.

At an Indian residence near the Mexican house a squaw standing in the doorway beckoned us to enter. She had in a store-room, back of the living-room, some small images of lava or malpais which she wanted to sell. They had been made, she said, by her husband and son, who chopped them out of the porous stone with a small hatchet. They represented the black bear, dogs, swans and geese, which are still worshipped by some of the old women of the pueblo, who generally keep them in hiding in the back rooms

COCHITI INDIAN.

Sight=seeing.

of their houses, though sometimes they are seen on the little mantels over the fireplaces.

There was also quite an assortment of articles which had collected for years. Flintlock guns used by the ancestors of the present owners, and many stone implements such as spear, arrow, axe heads, and old mortars and pestles cut out of lava. There were also drums and gourds and saddles of Navajoe work, covered with leather and ornamented with brass-headed tacks. Besides these there were saddles made in the pueblo, similar to our roping saddles, having pommels and rolls.

Having bought some of the stone implements from the woman, we started, laden with these and the saints, for the little adobe store, to get some necessary supplies previous to leaving Cochiti on the morrow. There are two of these stores in the pueblo, both kept by Mexicans, who supply the villagers with groceries, canned goods, cheap calico, harness, and other articles, which are always bought in small quantities, for no one, Indian or Mexican, has much money with which to purchase these luxuries, as they are considered. We bought quite a quantity of provisions, and were gazed at with interest all the while by the usual loiterer, probably on account of the unheard-of large sale the storekeeper had made to the strangers in the pueblo.

Returning heavily laden to our room, there came toward us into the pueblo a large bunch of burros driven by two Indians, who were bringing the animals into the village corral for the night. Raising burros is one of the principal occupations of the Indians in Cochiti. The animals are all herded together, and each person owning any in the bunch has a special day assigned on which it is his duty to care for the lot. The horses are cared for in the same way.

The Pueblos get most of their horses from the Navajoes, who make a special business of horse-raising and travel from village to village with droves of Indian ponies or cayuses, which they trade for beads that the Pueblo Indians make in great quantities. Four of these strings of beads will buy a horse. Five dollars will also buy a horse; but, strange to say, five dollars will not buy the beads. This method of financiering was quite contrary to any we had ever heard of, but it seemed to suit the Indians, who place a

Sight-seeing.

much higher value on beads than they do on money. This is probably owing to the fact that to manufacture them necessitates a great deal of tedious and hard labor. They are made of shells obtained from the traders, and are strung after holes have been bored in them with hand drills, then all together are ground in a circular form with a stone used for the purpose.

Our last day at Cochiti was spent taking a farewell look at the place, and in company with Mrs. Grozier we visited some Indian families. In a house not far from the school were two squaws seated on the floor, shelling peas, which the Indians eat raw, as we do fruit; they consider them a great luxury. The room itself had a very neat appearance. The mattresses and blankets which had been used to sleep on, the night before, had been rolled up against the side wall and were being used as a settee. In front of this were several old buffalo skins with very little fur left on the surface, showing that they had been trampled upon for many years. In the centre of the room, from the roof timbers, was suspended, by raw-hide rope, a papoose cradle, in which was a sleeping baby. The Indians are very fond of children, and especially

Among the Pueblo Indians.

of boys. When a woman is asked the sex of her child, if a boy, she will promptly answer "hombre," meaning man. If the little one happens to be a girl the mother is very slow to say so.

On the walls of the room were bows and arrows, some in course of construction, while others looked as if they had been used in killing birds and rabbits, a sport of which the Indian boy is very fond. They all handle the bow and arrow with great skill. The familiar Winchester and a belt of cartridges, together with little trinkets, such as beadwork necklaces, medicine bags and eagle feathers, hung on wooden pegs on the wall. Along one side of the room a long pole was suspended from the ceiling by a rope at each end, and over it were hung the bright-colored, zigzag-designed blankets which are obtained by trading shell bead-work with the Navajoes. The black squaw dresses, also of Navajoe manufacture, and buckskin leggins, and moccasins covered with beadwork and colored with ochre, were hung over one end of this pole. From the ceiling were suspended ten or eleven drums, which the Indian considers sacred.

The beating of the drum is not an uncommon sound

PRIMITIVE PLOUGHS.

Sight-seeing.

at any hour of the night in the pueblo, whether at a sacred meeting in the estufa or a gathering in the plaza. The Indian is very reluctant to sell these drums. In fact, we could not buy one at any price, although we tried at several places. When an Indian will not sell his blankets, pottery, beadwork, or dance costumes, it shows that he has plenty to eat and is thoroughly prosperous. Under these circumstances, if he should give a price on any of his possessions, one feels he ought to have a mortgage on the man's house before paying it.

At another house three squaws were making pottery in their skilful although crude way, by working the clay into shape by hand, guided only by the eye. The jars, after being rubbed and worked into shape, are allowed to dry slowly before baking, which is done in the bake oven in front of the house. These ovens are made of stone and adobe mortar and resemble in shape the old beehive. Many of the jars were artistically decorated with odd conventional designs, and one which we purchased had on the inside two broods of game-chickens and two game-cocks. The rooster figured quite prominently on much of the pottery, probably owing to the fondness the people have for the game of "gallo."

Returning to the school-house, we had lunch; and when the wagon had been loaded and the team hitched, we started out of the pueblo, Mrs. Grozier and the school-children standing in the doorway waving to us.

On the road beyond the river we met some Indian boys driving a herd of sheep and goats into the pueblo. As our supply of fresh meat was out, Juan selected a young lamb, intending to carry it in the back of the wagon, alive, until our arrival at Santo Domingo. He made the purchase, and the boys went on to the pueblo with the remainder of the flock.

A little further along the road was a tent filled with bales of alfalfa and used as a store for the benefit of the freighters who were hauling provisions and mining machinery from Wallace, a railroad town, to Eagle, a silver- and gold-mining camp west of Cochiti, in the mountains. In front of the tent were scales, on which two Mexicans weighed the bales before selling. When but a short distance from the tent

PENA BLANCA CHURCH.

Sight-seeing.

the lamb, not being fixed in very securely, fell to the ground, where one of the wheels passed over its neck, and Juan was obliged to get it ready then and there for the provision bag.

Pena Blanca, a little Mexican town, with neat-looking adobe houses along the one street of the village, was just south of the alfalfa tent on the road to Santo Domingo. The single store the place boasted of contained a United States post-office, and around the door of the building a crowd of idle young Mexicans had congregated. The most prominent object in the little town was the old church, in front of which was the graveyard enclosed by a low wall. From the centre of the enclosure rose a large wooden cross almost as high as the edifice itself.

As we journeyed toward the south and compared the country with that further north, a great difference was perceptible. The country grew more and more barren the farther we travelled, and, although on all sides in the distance could be seen lofty mountains with beautiful coloring rising majestically into the clear blue dome above them, yet we missed the trees that further north had made such a fine foreground for the ever-changing picture. On the way down we passed several freighters, and often old Mexicans driving two or three burros laden with wood were seen slowly plodding along the dusty road.

III.

LIFE AT SANTO DOMINGO.

LIFE AT SANTO DOMINGO.

THE distance between Cochiti and Santo Domingo was not so great as we imagined, and we neared the latter pueblo before sunset, passing Wallace, the railroad town, on our way to the Indian village. The green fields of corn and alfalfa surrounding the pueblo were in fine condition and indicated great prosperity among the natives. On the outskirts of the pueblo was the corral, where a large number of horses were being fed by two or three Indians.

We went to the home of an Indian whom we had met in Santa Fé, and who lived in the second story of a little house near the river bed. His room, which was nicely ventilated, had at one side an open fire-place large enough to have three meals cooked in it at one time. In the centre of the room our friend's wife was standing, swinging a papoose cradle in which a tiny baby was sleeping, while sitting around on the piled-up blankets were several squaws with little ones in their arms. We waited among this group until our friend returned from work in the fields, and told us he had a vacant house a little way up one of the streets.

Unlike the pueblos of San Ildefonso and Cochiti, where the houses face on a plaza or square, Santo Domingo is laid out in streets running parallel to each other. In the centre is one main thoroughfare, which the houses on all the other streets on either side of it face.

Reaching the house in question, we prepared our evening meal. In a short time several of the old bucks of the village called, and sat around, curiously looking at us as they talked with each other. Among our visitors was a young man, a cousin of the owner of the house in which we had located. He could speak a little English, and we gladly seized this opportunity of learning from him something about our

CORRAL AT SANTO DOMINGO.

Life at Santo Domingo.

surroundings. After taking out the little square of glass that formed the one window of the room (the Indians have windows for light, not ventilation), we questioned the young buck about the house, why such a nice-looking place was vacant, when so many people in the pueblo were huddled together in one room. He told us that about a year ago his cousin had died in the very room in which we were sitting, and that the place had been uninhabited since. On inquiring the cause of the man's illness, the fellow said, pointing to his chest, "He was sick here, and coughed all the time."

Not sharing with the Indian any superstitious antipathy to the place, but fearing there might still be some germs of the disease in the room that had been closed for so long, we decided to sleep once more in the wagon rather than to run any risk of infection.

Accordingly our bed was made up as it had been before. The night was very noisy, more so than any we had spent in Cochiti, for all the dogs (and Santo Domingo is noted for possessing hundreds of them) kept up a furious barking, seemingly selecting our street as a place to give vent to their feelings. We slept very little during the night, and when at last the place partially quieted down the first faint streaks of dawn were visible through a hole in the wagon cover.

Awakening at sunrise we were greatly surprised to see several pairs of eyes gazing at us under the canvas, from all directions. Seeing our covered wagon in one of their streets had, no doubt, aroused the curiosity of the villagers, and it was in this way they sought to satisfy it. How long we had been the centre of attraction is hard to say, but probably for some time; and even the fact that we were awake, and motioning them to go away, had no effect whatever upon them. In a few moments, however, Juan came up and told the crowd to stand by.

During the morning the men loitered around our doorway, talking and smoking. We were about to go around the pueblo, when, coming toward us from the river, were six bucks representing goblins. They were stripped, with the exception of a flannel breechcloth and moccasins. They wore false heads, perfectly cylindrical in form from the shoulders up, and with holes in front for the eyes. Four of them were painted black with white spots down their backs, and

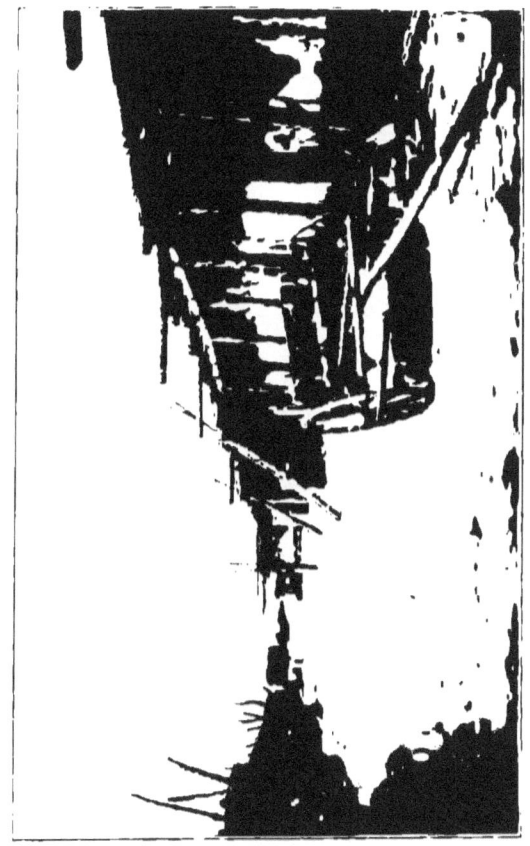

A STREET IN SANTO DOMINGO.

Life at Santo Domingo.

the remaining two, yellow with black spots. They wore armlets of rawhide in which were stuck corn husks. Some carried corn husks in their hands, while others had loaves of bread or tortillas. Thus arrayed they appeared in the village streets. They were supposed to have come from the river to make the men work on the bridge, which had been washed away by the spring freshets. The goblins ran through the pueblo from house to house, frightening in their march the children, who ran for protection to their mothers. They chased the bucks to the river, pointed out the place where they were to work, and made them commence the new bridge at once. The river bed at this point was fully a mile in width, while the stream itself was not over a hundred feet wide and the water at the deepest point reached about to a man's waist. The bridge consisted of quadrupods, made from the trunks of cottonwood trees, in which were placed faced logs, spanning from one to the other, crossing the river. The stream being so shallow the abutments were put in place without much difficulty by eight or nine of the strongest bucks, who waded into the water and put in place the timbers which the other

Among the Pueblo Indians.

men passed to them. The bridge was completed late in the afternoon, and on the return of the bucks to the village a large camp fire was started, around which, until a late hour, the men collected, resting, and evidently comparing their ideas of bridge construction.

During the evening we visited some of the people, who most cordially received us and showed us their possessions. In many houses Navajoe blankets were hanging around, also buckskin suits, and quivers made of mountain lion skin. Before turning in for the night we purchased two Navajoe blankets, and wrapping these around us, so that the dogs of the village would think we were Indians and not molest us, returned to the wagon. There was the usual barking of dogs together with a parade that moved through the village streets, making great commotion. The sound of the bugle, the governor shouting, and the beating of an old army drum, could be heard all at one time. The procession moved up and down the streets of the village, the sound becoming louder, then softer, and louder again, as its distance from us varied. Finally the little company approached us,

IN HOLIDAY ATTIRE.

Life at Santo Domingo.

and when passing we could distinguish by aid of the starlight a drummer on either side of the bugler, and all three marching in front of the governor, who was shouting at the top of his voice. They passed us; then, having gone the rounds, returned to their homes. This parade announced to the people that gallo was to be played in the main street the following afternoon. The drummers and the bugler were to attract the attention of the people while the governor made the announcement.

Leaving Juan to cook breakfast next morning, we went to one of the largest houses in the pueblo, where several families lived together. They had just commenced eating, and asked us to partake with them. Accepting the invitation, they handed us small stools, and we joined the circle. In the centre of the group, on the floor of the room, were two flat baskets, one containing dried beef and the other tortillas. We helped ourselves to these, and were each handed a cup filled with a black sour liquid called, by the Indians, coffee.

In our own room Juan awaited us with a well-cooked breakfast, which was thoroughly enjoyed, our appetites not being in the least impaired by the first course eaten with the Indians.

After breakfast we went with our landlord to buy another blanket and some pottery. One buck on whom we called had several pieces, including a large jar decorated in conventional design, for which he wanted three dollars. Visiting several other places in quest of a piece with bird ornamentation, we found that figure decoration was not characteristic of the Santo Domingo Indians. On making this discovery we hastened back for the piece before chosen, and imagine our surprise to find that during our absence the jar had increased in value one dollar and that the man would not for an instant consider his first-named price. This trait the Indians probably develop by coming in contact with traders who visit the Indian villages and buy pottery, blankets, and other articles of Indian manufacture, giving the poor, unsuspecting creatures about one-third the value of the articles in beads.

Having learned a lesson from our last transaction, we went in search of a blanket to a house not far from the one where the pottery had been made.

INDIAN HOME.

Life at Santo Domingo.

There were several blankets hanging around, but, as the owner wanted as much again for them as they were worth, he did not make the sale. Our interpreter told us that three strings of beads, such as the traders take into the pueblos, would buy a blanket. These beads we subsequently priced in Santa Fé, and to our amazement found that three strings cost just one-fourth the price the man had named for a blanket.

It had been our intention, at the start, to travel as far west as Laguna, a pueblo having a population of about one thousand Indians, and, being so far from Santa Fé, one very seldom visited by the whites, but the horses began to show signs of giving out, making this impossible. Had they been good ones we would have remained in Santo Domingo a week longer, to witness a large dance to take place at that time, and afterward travel further west.

Greatly disappointed at being obliged to shorten the trip, we returned to the house to prepare for our departure, and found Juan sitting on the back of the wagon, which he had loaded, talking with three young bucks with whom he had become acquainted during our stay in Santo Domingo. One of the group espe-

Among the Pueblo Indians.

cially attracted our attention. His straight black hair hung below his waist, around which he wore a Navajoe belt of oval silver discs. The silver buttons on his buckskin leggins were also made by the Navajoes. We levelled the camera and were preparing to take a picture of the group, when Juan informed the little company they were about to be photographed. This they would not have, and were walking away, when we handed them a picture of an Indian. Immediately they were all attention, and as they gazed at the picture the button was pressed unknown to them.

At the corral some bucks were getting the horses ready for the games of the afternoon; and as we passed along the road leading from the pueblo, wagonloads of Mexicans were coming from the neighboring settlements and from Cochiti to Santo Domingo to be present at the celebration.

We drove on through Wallace, hoping to reach Cerrillous, about ten miles beyond, by night; but this was not possible, as, travelling until sundown, our usual hour for striking camp, Wallace was still within sight. We drew the wagon up beside a little stream

Life at Santo Domingo.

—Cerrillous Creek the bed of which was covered with a limy substance, and found the water not good to drink, being full of alkali. After boiling, however, it did very well in coffee.

While preparing supper a young fellow rode up and entered into conversation with us. He had just left the mining camp at Eagle and was in search of work. Our meal was shared with him, and, inviting him to take breakfast with us on the morrow, we retired. Next morning our friend was nowhere in sight. He had probably taken advantage of the early morning light and ridden off on his lonely journey.

After breakfast we broke camp and proceeded up the road, which follows the railroad for about two miles; then, leaving the plain, we ascended the hill and were once more on the mesa. Looking backward, the road over which we had travelled from the Indian village could be plainly seen, and in the distance stood Santo Domingo Mountain, enveloped in a thin mist, but clearly distinguishable against the southern sky.

After travelling slowly for many hours, a little mining camp, with its derricks and shafts, appeared up in the hills. This proved to be the mines of Waldo, that supply the Santa Fé Road with coal. Here it was that we received our first information about the great strike that had tied up most of the western railroads, and on account of this strike the mines were not being worked.

Across the ridge, not far from the mines, was the little town of Waldo, a well-laid-out village with rows of neat-looking houses, the residences of the miners. Farther down the hill was the general store, which is under the management of the railroad company and supplies the people with everything in the line of groceries, dry goods, etc. We were greatly surprised to find such a store in a little mining settlement up in the hills of New Mexico, and also at the quantity and quality of the stock.

Cerrillous, a small settlement beyond Waldo, is a typical railroad town, with its small hotels and restaurants, billiard and pool rooms, saloons and stores. On our arrival in town several freighters whom we had met on the road further down were hanging around the feed store, talking over the news of the day with some of the townspeople.

Life at Santo Domingo.

As we had for the past two weeks heard absolutely nothing of the events taking place in the outer world, even this local gossip was welcome.

The most important topic under discussion was the scarcity of beer. The supply had given out several days before, and, on account of the strike, had not been replenished, causing a beer famine. Two trucks, however, had been sent to Santa Fé, and it was expected that relief would soon be at hand. In the course of conversation it was learned that the deputy sheriffs were organizing a posse to go to Raton to help move the mail trains that the strikers were holding back. This caused unusual excitement, and the figure of an armed deputy passing through the street was the signal for further speculation on the great issue at stake. Other and less important subjects followed these all-absorbing ones until our departure from the town, which was witnessed by a large proportion of the inhabitants, who had gradually collected in the vicinity of the store.

The cañon through which the road out of Cerrillous runs is very rough, large stones and deep gullies sometimes lying in the direct path of the traveller.

Among the Pueblo Indians.

The condition of the road and the horses prevented our going far, and we were obliged to camp for the night when only half a mile from town.

Realizing that the horses would never reach Santa Fé at this rate, Juan went to a little house, next morning, near the roadside, a short distance up the cañon, to see if he could procure a horse to take the place of our old black, which was nearly played out. He returned with the information that the people, who were Mexicans, would give us no assistance, although they had several horses grazing near the house. However, they told him that an American family lived a little way back from the road, over the hill. Trusting they would help us out, we walked in the direction named, and found a small cottage in among the trees. It was the home of one of the Waldo miners, who, being out of work, was glad to be of assistance to us. He hitched his team of sturdy mustangs to the wagon, and, with the wrecks tied on behind, the journey was continued up the cañon, which became narrower and steeper as we proceeded up the mountain.

The mustangs did good pulling over this, one of the

IN THE CAÑON.

Life at Santo Domingo.

worst stretches of road in the country, and we realized that the change had been made none too soon, for the cripples, being unable to keep up with the mustangs, began to hang back. Seeing that this was interfering with our progress, Juan cut the ropes and led them up more slowly. At the top of the hill it was found the black horse could go no further. So, tying him to a cedar tree near by, we left him, our driver promising to get the animal on his return next day and care for him until sent for by the owner.

Through Carmensville, a once prosperous but now deserted village, we passed. It was a desolate-looking place, its buildings gradually crumbling away by exposure to the elements and from want of repair.

From the top of the hill the old town of Santa Fé, our starting-point, was visible across the plain many miles away. The place appeared like a small dot at the foot of the mountains, and, looking toward it from our position on the hilltop, the winding road we were about to pass over could be easily traced across the sweeping plain.

The famous turquoise mines of New Mexico next

Among the Pueblo Indians.

came in sight, and the mountain containing them was resplendent in the sunlight that enveloped it.

At Bonanza, a little settlement of three houses at the foot of the hill, we partook of the last meal of the trip; then we started across the plain, and as the sun was sinking below the western hills we drove by the Indian school on the outskirts of the town and entered Santa Fé.

IV.
TAOS.

FROM SANTA FE TO TAOS.

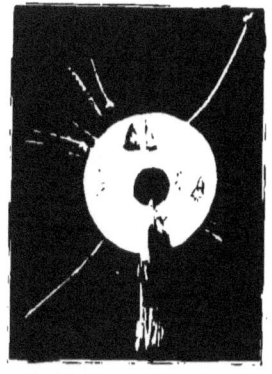

OUR entertainment by glimpses of Indian life, during the past two weeks, induced us to spend more time among the Pueblos before leaving New Mexico. Accordingly, Taos was selected as being a place of more than usual interest, both on account of its buildings and of the battle that had been fought at the pueblo during the insurrection of 1847, when the United States troops avenged the murder of Governor Bent.

Our plans were made during the following two days to visit Taos up in the mountains, seventy miles north of Santa Fé. We concluded to make this trip, not with a team as before, but by rail, on the Denver

Among the Pueblo Indians.

and Rio Grande narrow-gauge road to Embudo, and thence to Taos in the mail wagon.

With our blankets in the mail bag, the cameras, six-shooters, and a hand-satchel, we arrived at the station as the train drew up to the platform. The cars appeared very small, and the little wood-burning locomotive seemed to do a great deal of puffing, considering the slow rate of speed at which it travelled.

Our fellow-passengers were mostly Mexicans who kept up a steady flow of conversation in their foreign language, making it almost impossible to realize we were within the borders of the United States.

Travelling toward San Ildefonso, we had, from time to time, glimpses of the road so recently passed over, and in two or three places the exact spots of our camps could be distinguished.

At the rio the track entered the cañon, and followed the stream, which at this point flowed very swiftly over its bed of gravel. An old freight car, removed from its trucks and supported on piles, formed the station of San Ildefonso. It was situated some distance from the pueblo, which could be plainly seen from the car window. The sight of the little

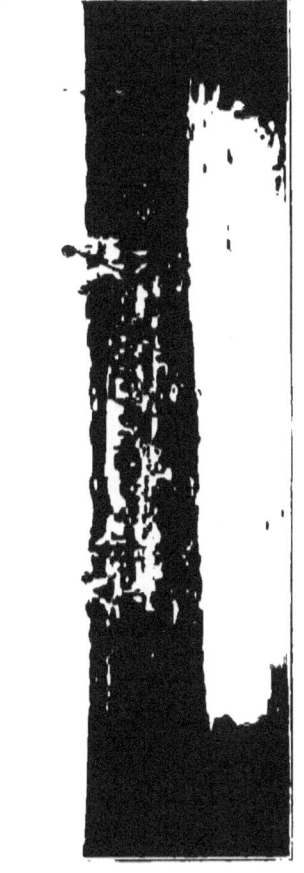

IN THE FIELDS.

From Santa Fe to Taos.

village brought back many recollections of our stay in the place, of the people, and especially of Juan, our late travelling companion, who would have enjoyed so much our present outing.

Passing the pueblo of Santa Clara, we stopped at Española, a railroad town, where quite a congregation of Indians and Mexicans had collected around the station. They were seated on the platform, conversing: the Indian women surrounded by pieces of pottery, which they tried to sell to the train's people. At the general store and post office, several teams and saddle horses were hitched. The store was filled with people, who evidently expected the train would bring the mail that had been for the past two weeks delayed on account of the strike.

At Española, several passengers boarded the train, which, as it moved in and out around ledges of rock, followed the irregular course of the stream. The river had the appearance of a clear mountain brook, of a beautiful greenish color, whirling around in deep holes, then bounding over large stones on its way down the rough rocky cañon. The roadbed here, where the spring freshets sweep away everything before them, is protected by breastworks of piles, to prevent it from being washed away.

The train slowly travelled along the up grade until noon, when we arrived at Embudo, where the railroad leaves the rio and ascends to the mesa. The mail wagon, in which we were to continue our journey, was at the station, awaiting the arrival of the train. Two mail bags from Santa Fé were thrown on the wagon, and these, together with ours well filled with blankets, made it appear that the strike was at an end, and the mails on the way to Taos.

The wagon was drawn by a pair of fat mustangs, and driven by a young Mexican who travels, under contract with the Government, between Embudo and Taos, a distance of thirty-two miles, and daily carries the mail between the two points.

We left the station a little after noon, the sun shining brightly on the surrounding hills. When a short distance up the road, however, a storm could be seen rapidly approaching us down the cañon. The heavy black clouds came nearer and nearer, and grew heavier and blacker as they approached, until it seemed as if they could no longer hold the water in them.

WEARY OF WORK.

From Santa Fe to Taos.

Then the rain fell in torrents, pouring in a cloud burst, and giving us barely time to cover ourselves with the almost empty mail bags before the storm was upon us. This protection, however, was not long necessary, for the fury of the storm soon spent itself, and the clouds, passing over the mountains, left the sky clear.

Rinconado, a little Mexican adobe town, was the first stopping-place, and at the general store one of the mail bags was left with the postmaster.

The road between Embudo and Taos was built by the Government for a mail route, at great expense and with much hard labor, as the country is broken up by high mountains and deep cañons. For some distance the road is cut in the mountain that forms the east side of the cañon. Above us, the hills, rising perpendicularly from the road, pierced the sky overhead; while on the other side, down in the bottom of the cañon, the rio flowed, swiftly eddying as it passed on toward the south.

The mountain side was almost barren, as, with the exception of some scrub cedar bushes, there was no sign of vegetable life. But what most forcibly strikes the eye of the traveller is the gorgeous coloring of the soil and rocks in the hills on either side of the stream. The soil blends from a deep red to lighter red and white, then into the greenish tint of the rocks that crop out here and there on the surface of the hills.

In many places in the sides of the cañon were large circular indentations, made at a time when the bed of the stream was much higher than it is to-day, and when a greater amount of water, constantly flowing, caused large boulders to grind these whirl-holes in the hard, solid rocks.

Leaving the cañon, the road goes over the hills, and along the roadside are mounds of sand, which show by the deep cuts and gullies in them that in time they will be entirely washed away by heavy rainfalls that frequently occur in the vicinity. From the top of one of these hills, the river again came in sight, and beside it, like an oasis in a desert, lay the little town of Cieneguiella, in a fertile valley of green fields and gardens.

From Cieneguiella we ascended to the mesa, five hundred feet above the town, and started over the wide plain bounded by distant mountains. Through

FATHER AND SON.

From Santa Fe to Taos.

the centre of this vast level plain the cañon containing the Rio Grande penetrates, cutting deeply for hundreds of feet below the surface. At the sharp turns and curves of the cañon, the course of the river, which looked like a thread, could be traced.

Another storm approached, travelling in a mass, and apparently following the course of the cañon. Before it reached us, however, the cloud burst and emptied its contents into the river below.

As we neared Taos the country became mountainous again. The hills were covered with sage bushes, and cedars of a much larger growth than those in the lower country grew side by side with them. We were fully eight thousand feet above the level of the sea, and could clearly distinguish the timber line on the mountains around us.

Just before sundown we drove through the town of Ranches de Taos, by the old church built over a hundred years ago, then on three miles farther into Taos; and as the sun was sinking in splendor behind the hills, our caravan arrived at the post office. Seeing our well-filled mail bag, the postmaster, thinking no doubt that the strike was at an end, rushed out to get it. Explaining to him that we held the key of the bag, and would show him the contents if he so desired, he was convinced it was not the property of the Government. In spite of this he looked quite crestfallen as we drove away to the adobe hotel near by.

The hotel, the mail carrier told us, was kept by a German, who, he assured us, had plenty of good Sante Fé beer, which, considering the distance it had to be brought, was considered a great luxury.

The German proprietor proved a most genial host, and, as he ushered us in to supper, soon after our arrival, we took the places assigned us at the table, where the other guests of the hotel had already assembled. It was a mixed company that sat around the board. The village doctor, a young man from the East, the black smith, the editor of the weekly paper *Taos Herald*, several miners, some gentlemen of leisure about town, our host and his family and ourselves the latest arrivals.

The table was in one corner of a large, bare-looking hall, at the rear of which a space was curtained off for the use of commercial travellers, and as the meal

progressed we could plainly hear them making sales to the storekeepers, who passed in and out through the dining-room on their way to and from the salesroom.

In front of the hall, beside the bar-room, was the hotel office, separated from the dining-room only by a light partition extending about as high as a man's head.

The hotel itself is a one-story adobe structure, built, as are most Mexican houses, around a small courtyard, upon which the rooms face.

Our first glimpse next morning was of the beautiful snow-tipped mountains glistening in the sunlight, with Taos Peak, which is twelve thousand feet above the level of the sea, towering above them all.

We decided to spend the day sight-seeing in the old town, and devote the remainder of our time to the pueblo. Our guide, the editor, told us many interesting things concerning the place, and pointed out the several buildings, the most prominent of which was Taos Bank, the only wooden structure in the town. Beyond the bank and near the post office was the house where Governor Bent was assassinated by a body of Mexicans and Pueblo Indians in 1847. The oldest house in the place, now roofless, was built about seventy-four years ago, and was the home of Kit Carson, whose tombstone in the little American graveyard east of the town marks the spot where he was buried. Opposite the printing-office was the little church of Our Lady of Guadalupe, with the priest's house and convent beside it.

In the court-room near by a case was being argued by Mexicans—and although we could not understand a word they said, it could be plainly seen that the affair was creating great excitement. The trouble originated from a quarrel between two Mexicans at a dance the night before, when the defendant had used his knife too freely on the plaintiff. Such cases are frequent in Taos, and are generally decided in favor of the party having the greatest number of followers.

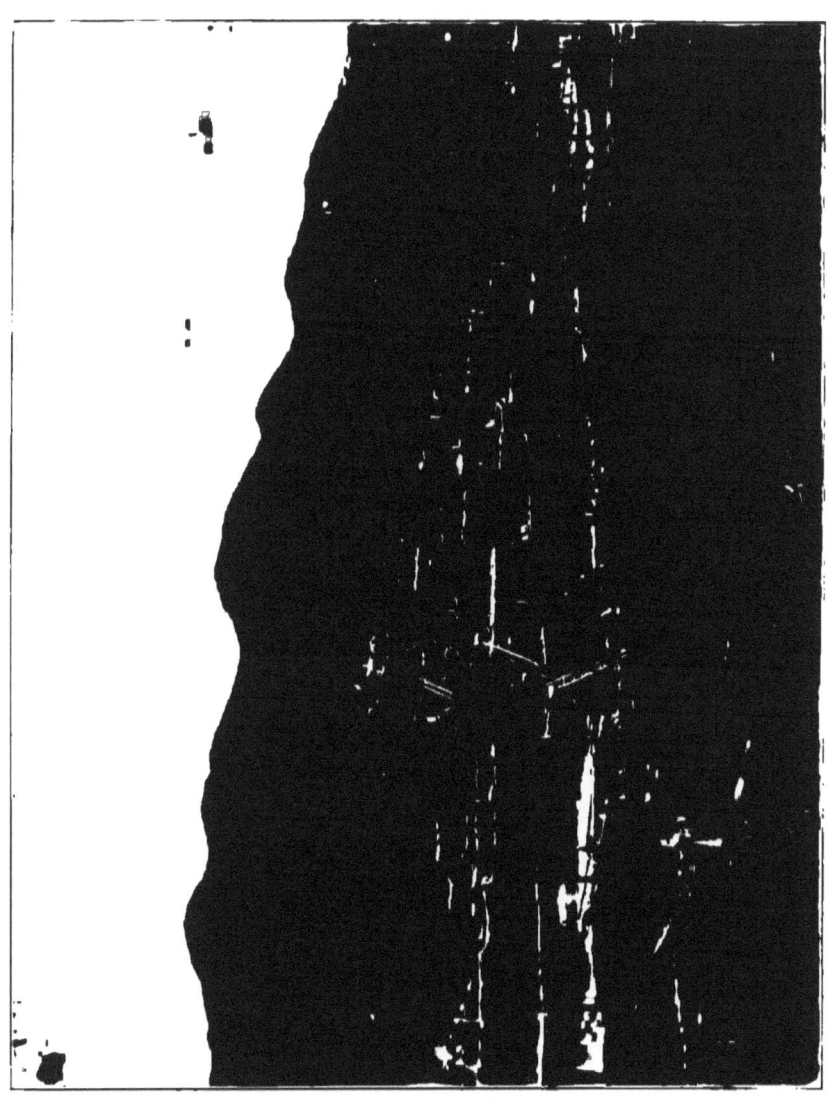

TAOS PUEBLO.

LIFE IN THE PUEBLO.

NEXT morning we made our first visit to the pueblo, driving out in a light wagon. On the road north of the town we met several Indians, who had walked over from the pueblo three miles beyond. These Indians bore a marked difference to those in the southern puebloes, both on account of their dress, which was purely Indian, without any Mexican innovations, and also by their features, which resemble more nearly the wilder tribes of the north. This change is, no doubt, the result of intermarrying with the Navajoes and the Apaches, who live but a short distance over the mountains toward the west. So long has this been going on that the Taos Indians have lost much of their Pueblo identity.

The morning was perfect, the clear atmosphere causing Taos Peak, with its barren top, to stand out boldly in the sunlight. Along the road, which, as we neared the pueblo, became very narrow, were fields of corn and alfalfa, and further along, on either side, was a growth of willows, so dense that even the sky above was not visible; all that could be seen was the side of the large mountain, at the foot of which the pueblo lies. Here and there an esaque crossed the road, carrying the clear water of Pueblo River into the fields of the Mexicans on the outskirts of the town. Leaving the willowy bower, there loomed up before us the two great pyramidal buildings of the pueblo, which, according to the historian, are the most interesting and extraordinary inhabited structures in America.

We went in search of a young Indian named Lorenzo, of whom we had previously heard. He was at home, and proved a most efficient interpreter and guide, as well as an agreeable companion. He was a well-educated fellow, having been graduated from Carlisle a year or two before. Since his return to the pueblo, however, he has been looked down upon by the rest of the inhabitants, who consider his knowledge a great disadvantage to them. He told us that on the day of his arrival home, after an absence of four years, a meeting had been called in the estufa

ESTUFA AT TAOS.

Life in the Pueblo.

to consider his case. The principal grievance was that he wore the clothes of a United States citizen instead of the buckskins of his brethren. He had been told he must change his manner of dressing, and on his steady refusal to accede to their demands they sought to force him to do so. When the council meeting had adjourned a committee was sent to tell him the decision arrived at; that he must either resign his American garments or be debarred from taking any part whatever in the affairs of the pueblo. He remained firm in his determination, and from that day has had no part whatever in the affairs of the community. There he lives, seemingly happy, in his little room with its modern appointments; his table well filled with books—his constant companions.

The two great buildings of Taos pueblo form irregular pyramids, being in some parts seven stories high, each tier or story covering a smaller area than the one below, to allow entrance from the roof. In each building over a hundred persons dwell; a whole family sometimes living in a little room near the top. Besides these structures a few small houses are scattered around the place, but the majority of the people live in the two main buildings. Near the most northerly of these are the ruins of the old church, with part of the adobe walls, seven feet in thickness, still standing. This church, during the revolt of 1847, was turned into a fortification, and held by Mexicans and Indians while being stormed by the United States troops, who marched from Santa Fé to Taos when the news of the murder of the Governor reached the Capital.

Concerning this battle Colonel Price, the commander of the American troops, writes as follows:—" Posting the dragoons under Captain Burgwin about two hundred and sixty yards from the western flank of the church, I ordered the mounted men under Captains St. Vrain and Slack to a position on the opposite side of the town, whence they could discover and intercept any fugitives who might attempt to escape toward the mountains or in the direction of San Fernando. The residue of the troops took ground about three hundred yards from the north wall. Here, too, Lieutenant Dyer established himself with the six-pounder and two howitzers, while Lieutenant Hessendaubel remained with Captain Burgwin in command of two

RUINS OF THE CHURCH.

howitzers. By this arrangement a cross fire was obtained, sweeping the front and eastern flank of the church.

"All these arrangements being made, the batteries opened upon the town at nine o'clock A.M. At eleven, finding it impossible to break the walls of the church with the six-pounders and howitzers, I determined to storm the building. At a signal Captain Burgwin, at the head of his own company, and that of Captain McMillin, charged the western flank of the church, while Captain Augney, infantry battalion, and Captain Barbar and Lieutenant Boon, Second Missouri Volunteers, charged the northern wall. As soon as the troops above mentioned had established themselves under the western wall of the church axes were used in the attempt to breach it, and, a temporary ladder having been made, the roof was fired. About this time Captain Burgwin, at the head of a small party, left the cover afforded by the flank of the church, and, penetrating into the corral in front of that building, endeavored to force the door. In this exposed position Captain Burgwin received a severe wound, which deprived me of his valuable services, and of which he died on the 7th inst.

"Lieutenants McIlvaine, Royall and Lackland accompanied Captain Burgwin into the corral, but the attempt on the church door proved fruitless, and they were compelled to retire behind the western wall. In the mean time small holes had been cut in the western wall, and shells were thrown in by hand, doing good execution. The six-pounder was now brought around by Lieutenant Wilson, who, at the distance of two hundred yards, poured a heavy fire of grape into the town. The enemy all this time kept up a destructive fire upon our troops. About half-past three o'clock the six-pounder was run up within about sixty yards of the church, and after ten rounds one of the holes which had been cut with the axes was widened into a practicable breach.

"The storming party, among whom were Lieutenants Dyer, Wilson and Taylor, entered and took possession of the church without opposition. The interior was filled with dense smoke, but for which circumstance our storming party would have suffered great loss. A few of the enemy were seen in the

TAOS INDIAN.

Life in the Pueblo.

gallery, where an open door admitted the air; but they retired without firing again. The troops left to support the battery on the north side were now ordered to charge on that side.

"The enemy then abandoned the western part of the town. Many took refuge in the large houses on the east, while others endeavored to escape toward the mountains. These latter were pursued by the mounted men, under Captains Slack and St. Vrain, who killed forty-one of them, only two or three men escaping. It was now night, and our troops were quietly quartered in the houses which the enemy had abandoned. On the next morning the enemy sued for peace, and, thinking the severe loss they had sustained would prove a salutary lesson, I granted their supplication on the condition that they should deliver up to me Tomas, one of their principal men, who had instigated and been actively engaged in the murder of Governor Bent and others.

"The number of the enemy at the Battle of Pueblo de Taos was between six and seven hundred, and of these one hundred and fifty were killed—wounded not known. Our own loss was seven killed and forty-five wounded. Many of the wounded have since died."

This battle, fought at the old church, was practically the end of the attempt to expel the Americans from the Territory.

In the thick adobe walls of the ruin, indentations, where cannon balls had been embedded, were visible. Lorenzo said that during his childhood his principal playthings had been the old balls fired by our troops during the battle.

From the old we went to the new church, where the Indians of Taos worship at the present time. The church, of course, is Catholic, but, coming less in contact with the Mexicans than those in the southern pueblos, the Taos Indians are not such strict followers of the faith.

The Indian, as a rule, has two religions; his original, which consists of worshipping the almighty chief, and also the Catholic, which was adopted from the Mexicans.

Many of the dances performed at the pueblos are merely forms of worship, or rather of prayer to the almighty chief. The planting dance, for instance,

TAOS CHURCH.

Life in the Pueblo.

that we had witnessed at San Ildefonso, was a prayer for the success of the crops. The hunting dance, also, is a prayer that the mountains and streams in the vicinity of the pueblos may abound in game and fish. Thus a sacred rite and an amusement are combined; and while the people enjoy it for the pleasure it brings them, they believe it will be the means of their further success.

The Indians are a very superstitious race, believing in all kinds of signs and workings of supernatural powers; sometimes avoiding contact with the most harmless things imaginable, fearing some evil influence may be exerted upon them.

A common form of superstition we had noticed was a belief that wearing certain charms would be a means of protection to the possessors. Accordingly many of the bucks wore in their belts small leather bags containing meal, in which were stones, carvings of malpais, pieces of turquoise, or old bullets. The meal is supposed to keep the articles pure and clean, and in constantly carrying them the wearer is thought to be proof against disease.

Lorenzo conducted us up the rickety ladders of one

of the great buildings of the pueblo. In front of most of the doors, on the roofs, little children were playing, sometimes perilously near the edge, while others were descending the ladders with great agility. From the top of this wonderfully built structure a fine view of the surrounding country was obtained. The cañon from which the little mountain stream comes bubbling down was before us, while toward the south, across the plain, lay the old town of Taos, with the marble-like peak at its side. All around, the high mountains towered into the azure sky, and at our feet were the fertile green fields in which the country abounds.

The field north of the building is kept under cultivation for the priest, who receives the products of the soil in payment for saying mass at the little church near by. The bucks, headed by the governor, were at work in this field, their garments floating in the breeze as they marched in file ploughing between the rows of young corn. When the work was completed, and the priest's acre in good condition, they shouldered their implements and marched on to their homes.

RETURNING FROM THE FIELDS.

Life in the Pueblo.

Wishing for a glimpse of the natural beauties of the surrounding country, we, with Lorenzo in the back of the wagon, started for the cañon. The morning was beautiful, the sky cloudless, and the bright sunlight, shining on the neighboring hills, harmoniously blended the varied tints of the earth with the deep blue of the sky. The road that follows the clear, sparkling mountain stream was very narrow, and the growth of trees on either side so dense that in some places the water, flowing some feet below us, was lost, to sight; then in the clearings, when the brook was again visible, trout could be plainly seen in the clear water that sparkled as the sun shone on it through the leafy bowers overhead.

A short distance up the cañon we came to a spot by the roadside which had been cleared of the trees that in former times had grown there. The clearing was circular in form, and covered an area of about one hundred feet square. This spot, Lorenzo said, was connected with the hunting dance, which occurs some time during the fall, when the elk are bugling in the mountains. The dancers attire themselves in costumes representing buffalo, deer, and antelope. A buck and a squaw wear stuffed heads of buffalos. Behind them are a pair of deer, who in turn are followed by the buck and doe antelope, and so on. The dancers repair to the mountain, and the dance begins on the circular spot by the roadside. In a short time a band of warriors is organized in the village to hunt the dancers, whom they capture and take down to the pueblo, where the hunters and the hunted join together in the great fall dance. The dance itself must be, from what we were told, similar to the one we had witnessed at San Ildefonso; the difference being in the costumes of the participants and the preliminary hunt in the mountain.

As we returned to the pueblo we could distinctly see a storm gathering over the Taos Peak, the top of which is usually of snowy whiteness. Since our trip up the cañon, however, it had changed into a grayish tint; and as we neared the town it seemed suddenly to grow black, as a great dark cloud, edged with feathery foam, came slowly over the top, and, spreading across the azure sky, hid from view the sun. Then the vivid flash of the lightning lit up the heavens, and, subsiding, seemed to leave them blacker

INDIAN PLOUGH TEAM.

Life in the Pueblo.

than before, while the deep roar of the thunder re-echoed throughout the neighboring hills. Then, amid the lightning flash and the rumbling of the thunder, the clouds emptied their contents over the country. Being of great force, the storm was not of long duration, and dispersed as rapidly as it had gathered, leaving the sky without a cloud. This midday rain is characteristic of the country, and during our stay in Taos each day brought a similar storm.

Next morning was spent visiting some of the people. Near the little bridge that spans the creek, several squaws were washing clothes in the clear water; while others were bathing little children, who, when the trying ordeal was over, lingered around, paddling in the shallow stream. In a potato field near by, some bucks were hoeing, having just begun their morning's work. They nodded pleasantly to us, as we passed on to one of the large buildings. We entered a room in the sixth story, occupied by a young buck and squaw. Besides the usual pictures of the saints, the walls of the room were decorated with bows and arrows; and a rawhide shield hanging on the door especially attracted our attention. We had

Among the Pueblo Indians.

tried to buy a shield in Cochiti, but without success. After our experience in Santo Domingo, we had taken precaution to purchase some beads that the Indians farther south valued so highly.

When Lorenzo told us the man was willing to sell the shield, we offered the beads in payment for it; but to our surprise he shook his head, saying he wanted money. All through this pueblo it was the same, and our bead currency proved worthless. We bought the shield at the man's terms; then, we visited one of the lower rooms, where a whole family were at home. Through Lorenzo we conversed with them, and tried to induce them to have a family group photographed on the little space before their door; but after great urging, only the father and boy could be prevailed upon to face the much-hated kodak.

During the evening one of the guests of the hotel called on us in our room. He was a man who had travelled extensively through the West during the early part of its history, and the many reminiscences of his life in the wilderness were very entertaining. At the time of his visit to us he was working a claim in Arroyo Hondo, a mining camp about twelve miles

ASTRAY.

Life in the Pueblo.

north of Taos. He invited us to take a trip to the mines, offering to let us dig and wash gold to our hearts' content; but as word had arrived that the strike was practically at an end, we decided to leave Taos in a day or two.

Accordingly our last visit to the pueblo was made the following morning. As we lingered around near the river, waiting for some bucks who had previously agreed to be photographed, there came toward us from the stream a small child carrying in both hands an old tin cup, with which he had been playing.

We levelled the kodak at the youthful subject, who, on seeing the camera pointed at him, stopped in his line of march and looked in amazement at having his escape cut off. As we stood by, afterward, to let the little one pass, his pent-up feelings gave way, and he cried as if heartbroken. His mother, a fine-looking squaw, at the sound of her child's cries, came from a house near by, seized the youngster by the hand and led him off, casting an angry backward glance in our direction.

We had previously heard that the governors of the pueblos would allow the children to possess but one dress, and had frequently noted the absence of this, the only wearing apparel of the little ones. On one occasion we came upon a very small boy at play, who was apparently suffering from the effects of a severe cold and sore throat. Not a vestige of clothing adorned the well-developed form of the little fellow save a good-sized piece of red flannel clumsily wound around his neck.

After photographing the bucks, who with Lorenzo had arrived soon after our encounter with our little friend, we bade all good-by and returned to town.

Having occasion during the afternoon to enter the plazuela around which the hotel is built, we saw quite a company collected at one end of the courtyard watching a little Indian boy dance. His father, a large buck from the pueblo, was seated in the centre, beating on an old tin pan and singing the usual Indian song, with peculiar nasal intonation. The boy had been dancing for twenty minutes, and after our arrival continued for fully ten more. When at last the dance ended he seemed perfectly exhausted, and fell in the arms of his mother, who was standing by proudly watching her boy.

HOMEWARD BOUND.

OUR trip to Embudo next morning was enlivened by the antics of a pair of young bronchos with which the journey was to be made. The load, consisting of five people, the baggage and a bale of hay, together with the weight of the wagon, was enough to warrant a slower rate of speed than that with which the young horses dashed off, but they seemed not to mind the weight in the least. At a sharp curve in the road the driver found it impossible to guide the horses around the bend, and the wagon was pulled over an embankment. The horses then started running over the plain, and in crossing a ditch the chain holding the body of the wagon on the truck snapped. Meanwhile the men of the front seat pulled on the lines, nearly drawing the wagon body over on the excited animals. When the horses finally quieted down, and the wagon had been pulled on the road, the driver fixed the chain with hay wire, and another start was made. The horses again rushed off at great speed, breaking the newly-repaired chain as we were descending a steep hill with a rocky incline on one side and a high embankment on the other. The only thing to save us from being dashed to pieces was to run the horses up the embankment, and in doing this we were almost thrown from our seats. Fully realizing that to continue the journey in this way meant certain death to the whole party, the driver returned to Taos for another team, and in about an hour a fresh start was made with a pair of sturdy grays.

When about ten miles from Taos three Indians rode toward us, driving a large bunch of cayuces. They stopped as they neared us, and, although we were not familiar with one another's language, they gave us to understand that they were Navajoes on their way to Taos to trade their horses with the Indians there. They seemed friendly, and were much interested in the kodak we carried, not objecting to have a picture taken.

When driving through Rinconado a large shepherd dog ran out of a house at the horses. Before

NAVAJOES.

Homeward Bound.

he could do any harm, however, one of the six-shooters came quickly into service, and with a yelp the dog whirled around in the road, like a pinwheel, and dropped dead at his master's feet. The man, a Mexican, on hearing the shot, had rushed out only to see his dog breathe its last. He threw both hands in the air and wildly shouted after us; but as our knowledge of Spanish was not very extensive, we could only by his actions gather the drift of his conversation. He was thoroughly excited, and his voice could be heard calling after us until the village was lost to sight.

Arriving in Embudo, we boarded the little train, and after a pleasant trip down the cañon reached Santa Fé.

With the mail that had accumulated during our absence was a letter from a Mexican lawyer, who had been engaged by the Jew from whom we had hired the old horses to deliver the following notice:

SANTA FÉ, NEW MEXICO.

DEAR SIR:—You are respectfully informed that there has been placed in my hands for collection a claim against you for seventy-five dollars, in favor of

Among the Pueblo Indians.

—— - & Son, of this city, for killing one horse. This claim is long overdue, and your creditor insists that the matter must be adjusted immediately, and I trust that you will at once arrange for its payment, saving thereby the trouble and costs consequent to a suit at law. Awaiting an early response,
    I remain, respectfully yours,
    ———— ————,
                    Atty.-at-law.

This letter was the first intimation we had of the demise of the old black, who in death was so much more valuable than he had been during his life—having been purchased by his late owner, we were told, five years before, for six dollars.

Refusing to comply with the polite demands of the Mexican and the Jew, we were summoned to appear in court the following week. Business of an urgent nature, however, necessitated our return to the East, and, giving bonds for a representative to appear, we left Sante Fé. A week later we reached New York—our trip a pleasant memory.

A new interest has been awakened in us by the Indian; his marked contrast to his white neighbors, his customs, many of which date back to the time when he was the sole possessor of the soil, and the great problem—his future—make him a subject of universal interest and of deepest thought.

With the beauty and grandeur of our great Western country, we were most forcibly impressed. Great sweeping prairies, majestic hills towering heavenward, and deep fertile valleys, all combine to make a harmonious and sublime picture that fills the beholder with awe and delight, and causes him to realize how wholly inadequate is his power to convey in a full sense a true idea of the wonders of the West.

www.ingramcontent.com/pod-product-compliance
Lightning Source LLC
Chambersburg PA
CBHW030818190426
43197CB00036B/594